W9-DES-293

✻ Smithsonian
A CIVIL WAR

BY STEPHANIE FITZGERALD

TIMELINE

CAPSTONE PRESS
a capstone imprint

Capstone Press
1710 Roe Crest Drive
North Mankato, Minnesota 56003
www.capstonepub.com

The name of the Smithsonian Institution and the sunburst logo
are registered trademarks of the Smithsonian Institution.
For more information, please visit www.si.edu.

Our very special thanks to James G. Barber, historian at the National Portrait
Gallery, Smithsonian Institution, for his curatorial review. Capstone would also like
to thank Kealy Wilson, Smithsonian Institution Product Development Manager, and
the following at Smithsonian Enterprises: Ellen Nanney, Licensing Manager;
Brigid Ferraro, Vice President, Education and Consumer Products; Carol LeBlanc,
Senior Vice President, Education and Consumer Products.

Library of Congress Cataloging-in-Publication Data
Fitzgerald, Stephanie.
 A Civil War timeline / by Stephanie Fitzgerald.
 pages cm. — (Smithsonian. War timelines)
 Includes index.
 Summary: "In timeline format, covers the chronology of major events of the Civil
War"— Provided by publisher.
 ISBN 978-1-4765-4156-3 (library binding)
 ISBN 978-1-4765-5176-0 (paperback)
1. United States—History—Civil War, 1861-1865—Chronology—Juvenile
literature. I. Title
 E468.3.F54 2014
 973.7—dc23   2013034174

Editorial Credits
Nate LeBoutillier, editor; Ted Williams, designer;
Svetlana Zhurkin, media researcher; Kathy McColley, production specialist

Photo Credits
Division of Military History and Diplomacy, National Museum of American
History, Smithsonian Institution, 38 (left); iStockphotos: duncan1890, 13 (right);
Library of Congress, cover, back cover, 1, 3, 4, 6–7 (back), 6 (left), 7, 8–9 (back),
8, 9, 10–11 (back), 11, 12–13 (back), 12, 13 (left), 14–15 (back), 14, 15, 16–17
(back), 16, 17, 18–19 (back), 18, 19, 20–21 (back), 20, 21, 22–23 (back), 22, 23,
24–25 (back), 24, 25, 26–27 (back), 26, 27, 28–29 (back), 28, 29, 30–31 (back), 30,
31, 32–33 (back), 32, 33 (right), 34–35 (back), 34, 35 (left), 36–37 (back), 36, 37,
38–39 (back), 38 (right), 39, 40–41 (back), 40, 41, 42–43 (back), 42, 43, 44, 47;
National Archives and Records Administration, Our Documents, 6 (right), 33 (left);
Newscom: Everett Collection, 35 (right)

Printed in the United States of America in Brainerd, Minnesota.
092013   007774BANGS14

TABLE OF CONTENTS

THE CIVIL WAR

In the middle of the 19th century, the United States was caught in a vicious struggle for survival. The bloody Civil War was unlike anything anyone had ever experienced before. The fighting was fiercer—the war casualties unimaginably high. As the brutal fighting dragged on for four years and the casualty numbers rose ever higher, it looked as if the United States of America would be torn in two. The promising experiment in democracy that had been started by America's Founding Fathers was on the brink of destruction.

After declaring independence in 1776, the 13 original British colonies won their liberty in the Revolutionary War and became the United States. But there were big differences between the North and South.

The South's economy was based on agriculture. Its wealth came from the export of cotton, which was produced on large plantations that were worked by slaves. The first black slaves in North America were taken from their homelands in Africa and transported to the New World on ships. Upon arrival they were sold. By the 1800s the majority of enslaved people were the descendants of slaves rather than those born in Africa.

The northern economy was based on industry—and it did not rely on slave labor. In fact, slavery was outlawed in most places in the North. During the 1800s the population in northern states grew rapidly as immigrants from Europe poured into the area. The immigrants provided the cheap labor that made the North such an industrial powerhouse. Many people opposed slavery in the North because it would take these low-paying jobs away from white workers.

In 1860 the number of slave states and free states were the same, giving both regions of the country equal representation in Congress. It was also a time of major expansion. The United States was gaining territory in the West, and the territories were being admitted as new states. Northerners didn't want slavery spreading into new states because it might upset the balance of power in Congress. Southerners didn't want slavery to be prohibited for the same reason.

The newly formed Republican Party was very vocal about wanting to stop the spread of slavery. When Republican presidential candidate Abraham Lincoln was elected in November 1860, several southern states felt it was time to declare their independence. South Carolina left the Union before the year was over.

By the date of Lincoln's presidential inauguration on March 4, 1861, six more states—Alabama, Florida, Georgia, Louisiana, Mississippi, and Texas—had seceded to form the Confederate States of America. The Confederacy then elected Jefferson Davis as its president. Before long the entire country would be embroiled in a bloody civil war.

This book presents a timeline of the most important events of the Civil War, from the events that led up to battle to the bitter end of the conflict.

THE ROAD TO WAR

March 3

The Missouri Compromise is passed in an effort to please both the North and the South. Missouri is admitted to the Union as a slave state on the condition that slavery is prohibited in any new states formed north of the 36th parallel.

Missouri Compromise

1781

1794

1820

Oct. 19

With the surrender of the British at Yorktown, Va., the American Revolution is effectively ended. The United States, which declared independence from England in 1776, is now a truly independent nation.

Eli Whitney patents his cotton gin. By simplifying how cotton is cleaned, the machine revolutionizes—and rejuvenates—the cotton industry. The gin allows cotton to be cleaned almost as quickly as it is picked, and a business that has relied entirely on slave labor grows extremely profitable at a time when it might otherwise die out.

Jan. 1

William Lloyd Garrison publishes the first issue of his Boston-based anti-slavery newspaper, *The Liberator*. Six years later Elijah Lovejoy, editor of the anti-slavery *St. Louis Observer*, is killed by a pro-slavery mob in Alton, Ill.

1828   1831   1852

July 4

Construction begins in Baltimore, Md., on the first railroad chartered in the U.S. The rise of railroads helps fuel industrialization in the North.

March 20

Harriet Beecher Stowe's anti-slavery novel *Uncle Tom's Cabin* is published. In one year it sells an unheard of 300,000 copies and spurs the abolitionist movement, a drive to end slavery that hastens the beginning of the Civil War.

THE FUSE IS LIT

May 30

The Kansas-Nebraska Act nullifies the Missouri Compromise, stating that the residents of each new state will decide whether it will be a free or slave state.

Nov. 6

Abraham Lincoln is elected 16th president of the United States.

Oct. 16

John Brown leads a raid on the federal arsenal at Harpers Ferry, Va. His plan is to arm slaves and start a rebellion. Brown's insurrection quickly fails. He is later convicted of treason and hanged.

April 12

At 4:30 in the morning, Confederate forces open fire on Union-held Fort Sumter in Charleston Harbor, S.C. The bombardment continues for 34 hours before Union forces finally surrender. The Civil War has begun.

1854 **1859** **1860** **1861**

April 20

The Gosport Navy Yard in Norfolk, Va., is destroyed to keep it from falling into the hands of the Confederacy. The 11 warships at the yard are burned and sunk, but Confederates salvage cannons and gunpowder and one sunken ship. The USS *Merrimack* is rebuilt as one of the world's first ironclad ships and rededicated as the CSS *Virginia* the next year.

April 15

Lincoln puts out a call for 75,000 volunteers to serve in the Union Army for three months.

April 17

Virginia secedes from the Union.

May 3

Lincoln calls for an additional 42,000 volunteers to serve for three years.

departure of volunteers from Dubuque, Iowa

GEARING UP
FOR BATTLE

May 6

Tennessee and Arkansas officially leave the Union.

May 20

North Carolina officially secedes. It is the 11th, and last, state to leave the Union.

1861

May 13

The British government declares its neutrality. The declaration allows for trade with the Confederacy but does not recognize it as a sovereign nation.

May 29

Confederates choose Richmond, Va., as their capital.

June

President Lincoln watches a demonstration of an early machine gun. The weapon, which is mounted on a two-wheeled artillery carriage, can fire 120 rounds per minute. Most rifles of the time fire at a rate of about three rounds per minute. The machine gun does not achieve widespread use in the Civil War.

Map legend:
- Union state
- Union territory
- Union border state
- Confederate state seceding before Fort Sumter, April 1861
- Confederate state seceding after Fort Sumter
- Border of Confederacy

June 18

The U.S. Sanitary Commission is formed to aid sick and wounded soldiers.

June 17

Thaddeus S. C. Lowe flies in a tethered balloon to show how useful the craft is for aerial observation. He uses a telegraph to communicate with President Lincoln from the air. Later in the war, balloons are used to report enemy movements and direct artillery attacks.

July 7

Two torpedoes are discovered in the Potomac River by the Union ship USS *Resolute*. The Civil War marks the first time in history that such mines are used extensively. By the end of the war, more than 40 Union vessels will be damaged or sunk by torpedoes.

THE SOUTH STRIKES

George McClellan

LIKE A ROCK

Early in the Battle of Bull Run, it looked as if the Federals—another name for the fighting men of the North—might overrun the Confederates. As southern soldiers began to retreat, Brigadier General Barnard Bee tried to rally the men. As he looked across the field, he saw a brigade holding their ground and firing furiously at the enemy. "There is Jackson standing like a stone wall!" he cried. "Rally behind the Virginians." The man he was referencing was Brigadier General Thomas J. Jackson—forever after known as Stonewall Jackson.

July 27

General George McClellan takes command of the main Union army, the Army of the Potomac, from General Irvin McDowell.

1861

July 21

Spectators come from Washington to watch the First Battle of Bull Run, in Manassas Junction, Va. The battle ends with the Union forces retreating in complete disarray. Union casualties total 2,896; 1,982 for the Confederacy.

Stonewall Jackson

"Here we heard of the terrible and disastrous battle of Bull Run, and a deep, burning shame crimsoned our cheeks at the defeat and disgrace of our arms." — Private Lucius Barber, Co. D, 15th Illinois Volunteer Infantry

Aug. 6

Officers in the Union Army realize that slave labor is giving the Confederate Army an advantage. In response, Congress passes the First Confiscation Act, which allows Union soldiers to seize any Confederate property during fighting. That includes slaves who are brought to war by their masters.

"One war at a time." — Abraham Lincoln, referring to the Trent Affair

Nov. 8

A U.S. ship stops the British mail ship *Trent* near the Bahamas. Authorities find James Mason and John Slidell, two diplomatic envoys from the Confederacy, onboard. The men are arrested and taken off the ship. The British are outraged. As a neutral party, they are allowed to offer passage to anyone who can pay. President Lincoln's Cabinet orders the men's release on Dec. 26.

Aug. 10

A southern victory at the Battle of Wilson's Creek, in Missouri, helps the Confederacy gain control of the southwestern portion of Missouri—a slave-holding Union state. The Confederates suffer 1,095 casualties in the fighting. Union casualties number 1,235.

GRANT
TAKES CHARGE

Jan. 20

Flag Officer David G. Farragut arrives in the Gulf of Mexico. His main mission is to capture New Orleans—the largest city in the Confederacy. Three months later, on April 24, he leads a fleet of 47 Union ships to capture the city.

Feb. 6

The Union Navy under Officer Andrew H. Foote captures Fort Henry on the Tennessee River.

1862

Jan. 30

The USS *Monitor* is launched at Greenpoint, Long Island. The *Monitor*, an ironclad ship, is one of the first of its kind. It is also the first ship in U.S. naval history to have a revolving gun turret, enabling it to shoot in any direction. Earlier ships had to line up next to each other in order to get a clear shot at the enemy.

Jan. 27

Tired of waiting for McClellan to act, Lincoln issues General Order No. 1: All Union forces on land and sea are to move against the Confederates on Feb. 22, George Washington's birthday.

> "If we had a million men, McClellan would swear the enemy has two millions. And then he would sit down in the mud and yell for three." —Secretary of War Edwin Stanton

Feb. 16

The Union Army under General Ulysses S. Grant captures Fort Donelson on the Cumberland River in Tennessee. The Union now controls two of the major water transportation routes in the Confederate West. Confederate casualties top 15,000 compared to 2,331 Union casualties.

THE NORTH FINDS ITS MAN

It was up to Confederate Brigadier General Simon B. Buckner, commander of Fort Donelson, to meet with Grant to discuss the terms of surrender. "No terms except unconditional and immediate surrender can be accepted," said Grant. "I propose to move immediately upon your works." This response earned the general great fame in the North, as well as the nickname "Unconditional Surrender" Grant.

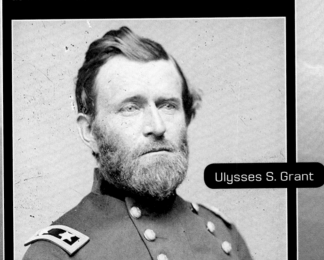

Ulysses S. Grant

Feb. 20

President Lincoln's 11-year-old son Willie dies from a "bilious fever," probably typhoid.

March 9

The USS *Monitor* and CSS *Virginia* battle in the waters of Hampton Roads, Va. It is the first battle of two ironclad ships in history. The Union suffers 409 casualties to the Confederacy's 24, but neither ship is sunk. The battle is a draw.

GENERAL LEE
TAKES COMMAND

April 10

The U.S. Congress passes a resolution calling for the gradual emancipation of slaves in all of the states. President Lincoln signs the measure.

April 16

Slavery is abolished in Washington, D.C.

Confederate president Jefferson Davis signs a conscription bill. Every eligible white male from ages 18 to 35 is to be drafted into the Confederate Army.

1862

April 6–7

The Battle of Shiloh, in Tennessee, ends in grisly death and carnage. Even though the battle is a Union victory, people in the North were horrified by the more than 13,000 Union casualties—2,000 more than the Confederates. They urge Lincoln to fire Grant. "I can't spare this man," Lincoln argues. "He fights."

Jefferson Davis

May 31–June 1

Although neither side can claim victory, the Confederacy suffers a loss at the Battle of Seven Pines, in Virginia, when General Joseph E. Johnston is wounded. Confederate General Robert E. Lee is given command of the Army of Northern Virginia.

May 10

The Confederates set fire to the Norfolk Navy Yard in Virginia before evacuating and moving northwest toward Richmond. Union troops occupy the city of Norfolk. The Confederate crew of the CSS *Virginia* blows up the ship after discovering it can't be sailed up the James River.

June 6

Union forces capture the city of Memphis, Tenn. The Mississippi River is now open to Federal traffic from the Gulf of Mexico to Vicksburg, Miss.

STRENGTH
OF THE SOUTH

June 9

The Battle of Port Republic, in Virginia, marks the end of General Stonewall Jackson's Shenandoah Valley Campaign. For 48 days Jackson kept Union forces away from the eastern front at Richmond while he racked up victory after victory. The campaign made Jackson a legend in the South.

1862

June 15

Confederate General James Ewell Brown "Jeb" Stuart leads his 1,200 cavalry troops on a four-day ride around the Army of the Potomac. Although the maneuver doesn't accomplish much in military goals, it causes Union General McClellan great embarrassment.

June 19

Lincoln signs a law prohibiting slavery in U.S. territories, which are lands held by the U.S. and occupied by its citizens but not yet states.

June 26–July 1

The Seven Days Battles are fought near Richmond, Va. Confederate spirits surge under the leadership of General Lee. Victory swings back and forth between the Union and the Confederacy as casualties top 13,000 for the Union and reach about 20,000 for the Confederacy.

July 17

Lincoln signs the Militia Act, which allows "persons of African descent" to serve in the Union Army and Navy. The act allows black men to serve, at first, in only noncombatant roles.

LEE'S NORTHERN INVASION

Aug. 19

Horace Greeley, editor of the *New York Tribune*, publishes *The Prayer of Twenty Millions*, in which he urges Lincoln to free all slaves. Three days later Lincoln responds not with anti-slavery legislation, but with an open letter to the editor. He writes, in part: "My paramount object in this struggle is to save the Union, and is not either to save or to destroy slavery. ... I have here stated my purpose according to my view of Official duty: and I intend no modification of my oft-expressed personal wish that all men everywhere could be free."

Aug. 26

Confederate cavalry enters Manassas Junction, Va. They capture the rail depot, as well as tons of Union Army supplies, which they begin shipping south. They also cut off communication to Washington, D.C.

Aug. 28–30

A Union defeat at the Second Battle of Bull Run at Manassas allows Lee's forces to cross the Potomac River into Maryland on Sept. 4. It is the first invasion into northern territory by the Confederate Army.

1862

Horace Greeley

W.M.Allison

Sept. 17

The Battle of Antietam, in Maryland, marks the bloodiest single day in American military history with 22,000 casualties. Clara Barton arrives on the battlefield with a wagon of medical supplies for the surgeons—who are wrapping soldiers' wounds with corn husks. She comforts the wounded with food, water, and her presence as bullets whiz around her.

Sept. 19

The Army of Northern Virginia begins its retreat across the Potomac River. McClellan doesn't pursue the battered troops, missing a possible opportunity to destroy the main force of the Confederate Army.

Sept. 22

President Lincoln views the Confederates' retreat from Antietam as a Union victory. It gives him the opportunity he's been waiting for to issue a preliminary emancipation decree. It states that unless the rebellious states return to the Union by Jan. 1, slaves in those states will be set free.

THE CARNAGE
CONTINUES

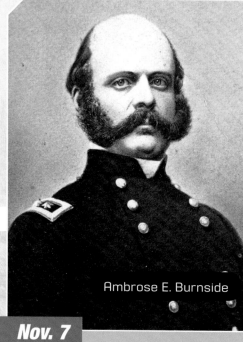

Ambrose E. Burnside

Dec. 14

General Burnside prepares to order another attack on Marye's Heights, but his officers talk him out of it. The Army of the Potomac begins its retreat to Falmouth, Va., where it will make its winter quarters.

Nov. 7

McClellan receives an order from President Lincoln dated Nov. 5. He is being replaced by General Ambrose E. Burnside.

The first black regiment in the Union Army, the 1st South Carolina Volunteers, is assembled. For the first time in history, African-American soldiers are recognized as part of the U.S. military. About 200,000 African-Americans will serve the Union over the course of the war.

Dec. 13

When Union troops arrive at Fredericksburg, Va., the Confederate Army is already in a strong defensive position on Marye's Heights. Lee's troops are lined up two deep behind a wall and occupy a large hill at the end of an open field. Any attack on the Confederate position is destined to fail. Nevertheless, Burnside launches 14 attacks. Not a single man makes it to the wall, and Union casualties top 13,000.

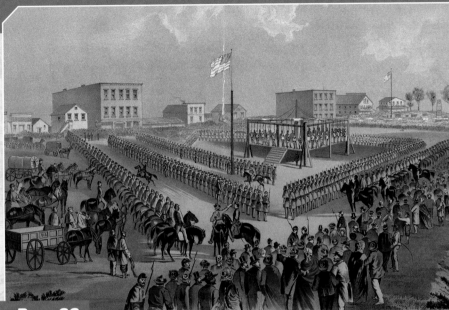

Dec. 26

The largest mass execution in U.S. history is carried out in Mankato, Minn., when 38 Native Americans are hanged in the wake of the Dakota Conflict, a violent confrontation between Dakota natives and white settlers. Some of the troops that captured the Native Americans had once been prisoners themselves. They were Union soldiers who had been released from Confederate prison camps.

Dec. 25

Union regiments stationed in Port Royal, S.C., spend Christmas Day playing baseball. Although the sport is relatively new, thousands of people in the area, also known as Hilton Head, take advantage of a rare break in the hostilities to watch the game. Some reports claim that 40,000 spectators attended the game between the 165th New York Regiment and members of the 47th and 48th New York, but the number has never been verified.

HOPE
FOR FREEDOM

EMANCIPATION PROCLAMATION

The Emancipation Proclamation was an executive decree abolishing slavery in the Confederate states. Lincoln's secretary of state, William Seward, commented: "We show our sympathy with slavery by emancipating slaves where we cannot reach them and holding them in bondage where we can set them free."

1863

Jan. 1

President Lincoln issues the Emancipation Proclamation. Finally, ending slavery is decreed as an official aim of the war. The proclamation also serves to keep England and France, both countries where slavery is banned, from joining with Confederate forces. In light of Lincoln's proclamation, supporting the South would mean supporting slavery.

Jan. 26

Major General Joseph Hooker takes command of the Army of the Potomac from General Burnside.

March 3

Lincoln signs a conscription act, which makes all male citizens from ages 20 to 45 eligible for military draft.

May 2–4

A Confederate victory at the Battle of Chancellorsville, Va., comes with a heavy price. Stonewall Jackson—Lee's most trusted and talented general—is returning from a scouting mission when Confederate troops mistake him and his men for a Union patrol. Jackson is shot three times. Southern morale takes a serious hit when Jackson perishes of his wounds May 10.

1863

The Robert Gould Shaw and the 54th Regiment Memorial in Boston, Massachusetts

May 13

The 54th Massachusetts is the first unit of African-American soldiers to be raised in the North. In addition to its other terms, the Emancipation Proclamation had made it legal for black men to enter the armed forces as soldiers. Among the recruits are Charles and Lewis Douglass, sons of escaped slave and famous abolitionist statesman Frederick Douglass.

RIGHT TO FIGHT

Frederick Douglass was an escaped slave and a leading abolitionist. From the start of the conflict, he had been urging Lincoln to let African-Americans fight in the war, which he considered a first step toward greater rights. He said, "Once let the black man get upon his person the brass letter, U.S., let him get an eagle on his button, and a musket on his shoulder and bullets in his pocket, there is no power on earth that can deny that he has earned the right to citizenship."

May 22

Union troops under General Grant begin the siege of Vicksburg, Miss. For six weeks Union boats lob mortars into the city 24 hours a day.

June 9

General Lee tries to capitalize on his victory at Chancellorsville by staging another invasion of the North. This time he sets his sights on Pennsylvania. Union and Confederate cavalry clash at the Battle of Brandy Station, in Virginia, as the southern army begins its trek north.

June 13–15

Lee orders his troops to clear the Shenandoah Valley of any Union opposition. In the Second Battle of Winchester, in Virginia, Confederates overtake the Union garrison; more than 2,400 soldiers surrender. The victory leaves the path to Pennsylvania clear for the southern army.

June 15

Realizing that the Confederate Army is heading into northern territory, President Lincoln calls for 100,000 militiamen from Maryland, Ohio, Pennsylvania, and West Virginia to protect against the invasion.

1863

June 28

Major General George Gordon Meade assumes command of the Union's Army of the Potomac. One of Meade's primary concerns is pinpointing the actual whereabouts of the Confederate Army.

July 1–3

Over the course of the three-day Battle of Gettysburg, the advantage changes sides many times. General Lee tries to end the battle once and for all with an attack on the Union center on July 3. The attack, known as Pickett's Charge, results in heavy casualties for Lee's army. The three-day casualty toll was staggering: 23,000 Union soldiers killed, wounded, or missing; 28,000 for the Confederates.

July 2

Jeb Stuart and his large cavalry finally return from a scouting mission ride around the Union armies, started eight days prior. The battle at Gettysburg has already begun. Some blame Stuart's late arrival as a major contributing factor for the South's loss at Gettysburg.

June 30

The Union cavalry under General John Buford rides into Gettysburg, Pa. Buford learns that his 2,700 men have ridden between two very large portions of the Army of Northern Virginia. He gets a message to Meade in Taneytown, Md.: "Send help fast."

negotiation of Confederate surrender between Grant (left) and Pemberton

1863

July 4

In the West the Confederates under General John C. Pemberton surrender to General Grant at Vicksburg, Miss. The Union now has control of the Mississippi River. The Confederacy in the East is cut off from its troops and supplies west of the river.

July 5

The Confederate Army of Northern Virginia begins its retreat from Pennsylvania. To the dismay of President Lincoln, Meade does not pursue the broken and battered army.

July 13–16

Anti-draft riots in New York City cause the deaths of 120 people—mostly African-Americans—including some children. Union soldiers returning from the Battle of Gettysburg are sent to restore order.

Aug. 21

A group of southern sympathizers led by the outlaw William C. Quantrill attacks the town of Lawrence, Kan., which was loyal to the Union. The raiders kill about 150 men and boys, and they loot and burn the town.

July 18

The 54th Massachusetts Infantry Regiment leads the assault on Fort Wagner, S.C. Half of the men in the regiment are killed in brutal hand-to-hand fighting. The attack finally becomes a Union siege. Confederate forces hold out for almost two months, finally abandoning the fort the night of Sept. 6.

Sept. 18–20

The Battle of Chickamauga, in Georgia, is fought for control of Chattanooga, Tenn. Gaining control of the city is important because the railroad center is considered the gateway to the heart of the Confederacy—the Deep South. Although the Confederates' 18,454 casualties were about 2,000 higher than that of the Union, the southern army manages to hold the town. Three days later the 11th and 12th Corps of the Army of the Potomac are sent to support the Union troops in Chattanooga.

THE UNION ARMY
REORGANIZES

William T. Sherman

Oct. 3

President Lincoln makes Thanksgiving an annual national holiday.

Oct. 18

General Grant is given command of all Union forces from the Mississippi River east to the Cumberland Mountains. In the western theater, General William T. Sherman takes Grant's place as commander of the Army of the Tennessee.

Oct. 26

Union ironclads and batteries on shore bombard Fort Sumter. Confederate defenders refuse to surrender. Despite bombardment that will last several days, the fort will remain under Confederate control until February 1865.

Nov. 23–25

The Union Army has been under siege at Chattanooga since the end of September. Sherman arrives with four divisions in mid-November, opening up a much-needed supply line, and the Union troops go on the offensive. After the Confederates are pushed out in the Third Battle of Chattanooga, the city will serve as Sherman's base of operations for the 1864 Atlanta campaign.

> Executive Mansion,
>
> Washington, _____, 186_.
>
> Four score and seven years ago our fathers brought
> forth, upon this continent, a new nation, conceived
> in liberty, and dedicated to the proposition that
> "all men are created equal"
>
> Now we are engaged in a great civil war, testing
> whether that nation, or any nation so conceived,
> and so dedicated, can long endure. We are met
> on a great battle field of that war. We have
> come to dedicate a portion of it, as a final rest-
> ... for those who died here, that the nation

Nov. 19

Lincoln delivers his Gettysburg Address at the dedication of the National Soldiers' Cemetery at the battle site. He states that the war is being fought to preserve a nation that was founded on the belief that all men are created equal. Lincoln was not the primary orator—and his concise speech of 273 words was much shorter than the two-hour speech given by educator and politician Edward Everett. Yet the Gettysburg Address is considered one of the most important, and most famous, speeches in U.S. history.

Feb. 1

Lincoln calls for an additional 500,000 men to be drafted in March for a three-year stint.

1864

Feb. 14–20

Union troops under General Sherman occupy Meridian, Miss. For five days the men destroy everything of value, including railroads, supply depots, arsenals, and warehouses.

Feb. 27

Federal prisoners of war, most of them sick or wounded, are transferred to Andersonville Prison in Georgia. During the 14 months the cramped, unsanitary camp is in existence, 45,000 Union prisoners are held there. Almost 13,000 of them will die.

March 12

After suffering a series of generals who seem reluctant to fight, Lincoln gives General Grant command of all the Union armies. Grant makes his headquarters with the Army of the Potomac.

April 9

Grant issues orders to Meade: "Lee's army will be your objective point. Wherever Lee goes, there you will go also." Grant is determined to continually harass the Army of Northern Virginia until it is worn down.

April 12

The Battle of Fort Pillow, Tennessee, is surrounded by controversy. Union reports state that the Federal Army was quick to surrender. It was reported that the majority of casualties, including the deaths of most of the more than 250 African-American troops stationed there, happened *after* the surrender.

DEEP WOUNDS

INJURIES MOUNT

Both the Union and Confederate armies suffered staggering losses at the Wilderness and Spotsylvania Court House battles. But the losses took a greater toll on the Army of Northern Virginia, which had fewer men to start with. The Confederates also had fewer men to reinforce their devastated troops.

May 8–12

The Battle of the Wilderness, which had been raging days earlier, erupts again nearby in the Battle of Spotsylvania Court House, in Virginia. Grant's decision to continue on the offensive after heavy losses at the Wilderness marks the first time the Army of the Potomac doesn't retreat or stay inactive after an important battle. The week-long casualty list reaches 18,000 for the Union Army and 12,000 for the Confederates.

May 31–June 12

Delays by the Union Army on the second day of fighting at the Battle of Cold Harbor, in Virginia, give Confederate forces a chance to build heavily fortified defenses. When the time comes to attack, Union troops march straight into a series of interlocking Confederate trenches amidst fields of fire. There is no place to hide from Confederate bullets. Many soldiers, remembering the massacre at Fredericksburg, assume they will not make it out alive. Union casualties reach 13,000 compared to the Confederacy's 2,500.

June 15–18

The Union's unsuccessful assault on Petersburg, Va., leads to a nine-month siege of the city.

June 3

Anticipating the carnage to come at Cold Harbor, a soldier from Massachusetts writes in his diary: "June 3, 1864, Cold Harbor, Virginia. I was killed." It was his final entry.

July 22

The Union inflicts heavy casualties on the Confederates in the Battle of Atlanta, in Georgia. At the end of fighting, Union casualties reach more than 3,500 with Confederate casualties numbering 8,500. The Union Army holds the city.

THE BEGINNING
OF THE END

July 30

Union forces try to break the siege of Petersburg in the Battle of the Crater. After digging a tunnel and blowing a hole in the city's defenses, Union soldiers surge in, only to be slaughtered in the crater. Union casualties reach 5,300 compared to 1,032 Confederate casualties. The siege continues.

Sept. 1

Sherman's Union forces take over the evacuated city of Atlanta. In the days preceding evacuation, General John B. Hood's retreating Confederate forces blow up railroad yards and munitions dumps on their way out of town. This ensures that Union troops won't be able to use the railroad equipment and the ammunition and explosives stored at the dumps.

1864

Union cap

Oct. 9

Sherman sends a telegram to General Grant, advising him of his plans for Georgia. He writes, in part: "Until we can repopulate Georgia it is useless to occupy it, but utter destruction of its roads, houses, and people will cripple their military resources. ... I can make the march and make Georgia howl."

Oct. 19

A clear Union victory at the Battle of Cedar Creek, in Virginia, finally breaks the Confederate Army in the Shenandoah Valley.

PRIME REAL ESTATE

The Shenandoah Valley, located in the northwestern region of Virginia, played an important role in the Civil War. In the very beginning of the war, General Stonewall Jackson's Shenandoah Valley campaign secured the area for the Confederacy. The Union's victory there in 1864 contributed to the Confederate Army's final destruction.

Nov. 8

Lincoln is re-elected president of the United States.

CRIPPLING THE SOUTH

Nov. 12

Sherman orders his men to destroy everything but homes and churches, and then leaves Atlanta on his "March to the Sea." For more than a month, the general will lead 60,000 soldiers on a 285-mile (459-kilometer) march from Atlanta to Savannah, Ga., leaving destruction in their wake.

Dec. 11

Sherman lays siege to Savannah. The Confederates abandon the city to Union forces on Dec. 20.

Jan. 16

President Lincoln receives a letter from President Davis suggesting a negotiated peace between two nations—not a reunification of the United States. Lincoln turns down the offer. He writes a response in which he states his willingness to discuss a peace agreement, as long as it deals with "our one common country."

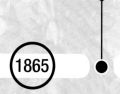

1864

1865

Dec. 22

Sherman sends a telegram to President Lincoln: "I beg to present you as a Christmas gift, the city of Savannah, with one hundred and fifty heavy guns and plenty of ammunition, also about twenty-five thousands bales of cotton."

Jan. 31

The U.S. House of Representatives passes the 13th Amendment to the Constitution to abolish slavery. It becomes law nearly a year later, on Dec. 6, 1865, after two-thirds of the states approve it.

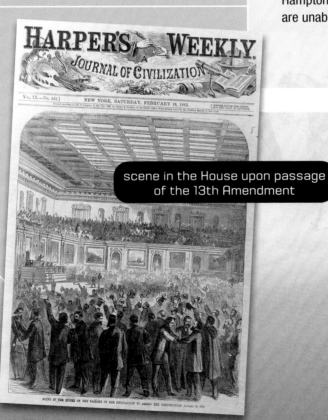

scene in the House upon passage of the 13th Amendment

Feb. 3

Lincoln meets with Confederate Vice President Alexander Stephens and others for a peace conference at Hampton Roads, Va. The two sides are unable to come to terms.

Feb. 19

Confederates abandon the city of Charleston, S.C. Union forces are regaining more and more territory.

Feb. 17

The mayor of Columbia, S.C., surrenders the city to Sherman's troops.

Feb. 22

The Confederate Army destroys its stores in Wilmington, N.C., and evacuates the city.

SEARCHING FOR PEACE

March 3

The U.S. War Department establishes the Bureau of Refugees, Freedmen, and Abandoned Lands. The agency will supervise all relief—food, medicine, clothing—and educational services for refugees and former slaves.

March 4

Inauguration ceremonies for President Lincoln take place in Washington. "With malice toward none; with charity for all ... let us strive on to finish the work we are in ... to do all which may achieve and cherish a just, and a lasting peace, among ourselves, and with all nations," Lincoln says.

1865

April 3

The Richmond, Va., arsenal is set on fire and destroyed. The Confederate Army also destroys the city's business district, bridges, and all army stores. Federal forces enter the burning city and claim it for the Union.

April 9

Lee surrenders his Confederate Army to Grant at the village of Appomattox Court House in Virginia. Lee tells his troops: "After four years of arduous service marked by unsurpassed courage and fortitude, the Army of Northern Virginia has been compelled to yield to overwhelming numbers and resources."

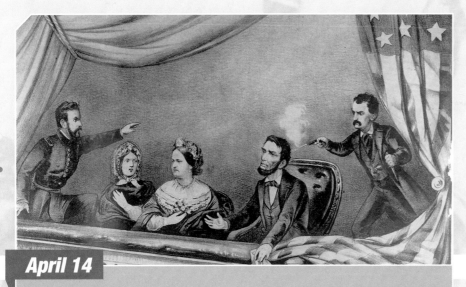

June 23

General Stand Watie and his Cherokee Indian forces become the last Confederate troops to surrender in what is now Oklahoma. The Civil War is officially over.

April 14

John Wilkes Booth assassinates President Lincoln during the play *Our American Cousin* at Ford's Theatre in Washington, D.C. Vice President Andrew Johnson subsequently becomes president.

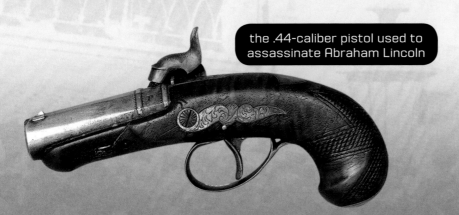

the .44-caliber pistol used to assassinate Abraham Lincoln

May 10

Jefferson Davis is captured near Irwinville, Ga. He is later charged with treason and imprisoned at Fort Monroe, Va., for two years. He dies in New Orleans, La., on Dec. 6, 1889.

THE PRICE OF PRESERVATION

The Civil War was finally over. The Union was preserved, but at a price. More than 620,000 soldiers and 100,000 civilians died in the bloody conflict.

The South, where most of the fighting took place, was economically devastated. Farms and plantations that had provided food—and wealth—to the region were destroyed. Livestock was slaughtered, and cities were reduced to piles of rubble. Buildings, bridges, and railroad tracks were in ruins—and there was no money to rebuild them. All over the South, people were homeless. Thousands starved to death.

In addition to the physical hardships, many people in the South found it nearly intolerable to accept defeat. Many southern whites found it hard to believe that their slaves were now free and theoretically their equals.

Before his death President Lincoln had been working on a reconstruction plan—a way to reunify the country as quickly, as justly, and as painlessly as possible. Some people in the government felt that Lincoln's plan was too easy on the rebels. After Lincoln's assassination the point became moot. Vice President Andrew Johnson, a southern Democrat from North Carolina, would be in charge of reconstruction.

Before the war northerners and southerners had been divided by economic and political differences. Many southerners felt a bitter hatred toward northerners who had destroyed their way of life. They resented the northerners who—they felt—came south after the war to take advantage of their weakened position. They felt hostile toward those who worked to improve the economic and social position of the newly freed slaves. Even though the war was over, the divide between North and South seemed to grow ever wider.

GLOSSARY

abolished—done away with

armory—a place where weapons are stored or soldiers are trained

arsenal—a place where weapons and ammunition are made or stored

artillery—large guns, such as cannons

bombardment—an attack of heavy fire from large guns

casualties—people missing, taken prisoner, injured, or killed

commission—a position in the military

conscription—forced enrollment in the military

envoy—a representative or messenger sent from one government to another

mortar—a short cannon that shoots shells high into the air

munitions—military equipment and supplies, especially weapons and ammunition

mustered—assembled in a group

reconnaissance—a mission to survey enemy territory to gather information

reinforcements—extra troops sent to strengthen a unit

secede—to withdraw from a group

siege—placement of an army around a location in order to cut off its supplies and force its surrender

READ MORE

Benoit, Peter. *The Civil War.* Danbury, Conn.: Children's Press, 2011.

Fitzgerald, Stephanie. *The Split History of the Battle of Gettysburg.* North Mankato, Minn.: Compass Point Books, 2014.

History Colorado. *A Civil War Scrapbook: I Was There Too!* Golden, Colo.: Fulcrum Publishing, 2012.

INTERNET SITES

Use FactHound to find Internet sites related to this book.
All of the sites on FactHound have been researched by our staff.

Here's all you do:

Visit *www.facthound.com*

Type in this code: 9781476541563

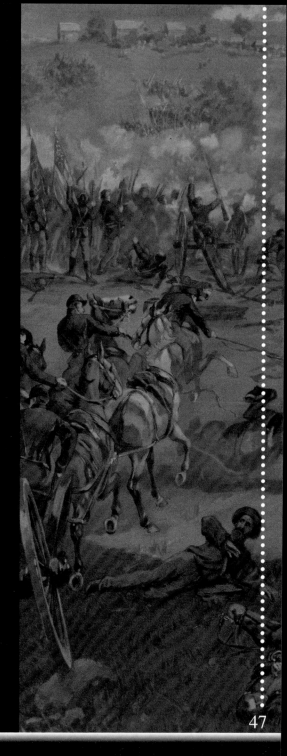

INDEX